Making Peace With Your Stuff

. . . because you probably WON'T need it someday

Kater Leatherman

Cover design and image
by Kater Leatherman

Author photograph on the back
by Karen Guay

Formatting by Candace Nikiforou

Kiwi Publishing
First printing, May 2012
ISBN: 978-0-9786136-2-4

Note: This book is written as a source of information,
not a substitute for professional advice.

Also by Kater Leatherman

THE LIBERATED BABY BOOMER:
Making S P A C E for Life

To order Kater's books, go to
www.katerleatherman.com

To contact Kater, email
katerleatherman@gmail.com

For my mother, who modeled good housekeeping, and my father, who instilled in me the habit of putting things back where I found them.

To Kristan Leatherman and Patrick Giammarise, thank you for inspiring me to write this book.

And, to my clients, for their courage to change.

*Thinking we might need something someday
is a story we tell ourselves to avoid the pain
of having to let it go.*

Introduction

It took me one month to write this book, compiled from my first book, *The Liberated Baby Boomer,* the column that I write for *The Annapolis Capital* and over ten years' experience as a professional organizer and home stager.

All too often, things that are no longer useful, wanted or liked are kept because we might need them someday. This protects us from the uncertainties of the future or, if it is too painful to let go of our object memories, stuck in the past.

One way to make peace with your stuff is to live with the things that you love now, that fit you now, that align with your lifestyle now because now is where life happens.

Since most of us don't have time to read paragraphs of information, this book is a condensed version of what I have come to believe - that changing your mind about your stuff will change your life.

There's nothing wrong with possessions
when they fulfill their purpose. . .
to bring enjoyment,
inspire us and enhance our lives.
But when they come between us
and our soul's longing for peace,
then aren't we postponing our desire to live fully?

Contents

In order to have what you want,
you have to make s p a c e for it.

What do you want?

Balance. . . less stress. . . more s p a c e. . .
. . . a sense of accomplishment. . .
. . . living liberated. . . a home sanctuary?

Three steps to attracting what you want:

1. First, declare what it is that you want.

2. Make every decision align with what you want.

3. Stay focused on what you want.

While keeping an eye on what you want,
what small thing can you do today that will support it?
Would it be cleaning out a junk drawer,
contacting someone to come and get their stuff,
hiring a professional organizer,
taking a load of stuff to the donation center?

Sometimes, letting go of an object
is a process that requires multiple steps.

*Assuming that your family and pets are safe,
if your house were on fire and
you had two minutes to grab five things,
what would you take?*

Why we keep stuff

Conditioning

We think it has value

Fear that something bad will happen if we let it go

To quell loneliness, anxiety and depression

Can be an effective distraction

There's pride in ownership

It feels like people "live on" in objects

Things can define who we are

We might need it someday

Fear of loss

Knowing "why" we keep stuff is good information,
but it isn't enough to affect change.
It's the "what" that matters. . .
as in what are you going to do about it?
The "what" is the action step that generates results.

*Is any one possession
worth your personal freedom?*

Consequences
of having too much stuff

C.H.A.O.S.
(Acronym: **C**an't **H**ave **A**nyone **O**ver **S**yndrome)

Debt

Stress and anxiety

Time robber when you can't find stuff

Strained relationships

Shame and embarrassment

Waste of our natural resources

Is your stuff insulating you from intimacy,
protecting you from feeling bored,
preventing you from moving forward in your life?
It's serving you in some way;
otherwise, you wouldn't have so much stuff.

*Is your home a storage s p a c e
or a living s p a c e?*

The dreaded "C" word

Clutter is nothing more than postponed decisions.

Clutter is dense energy that keeps you stuck.

There is no spiritual design for clutter;
therefore, clutter is anything that keeps you
from enjoying life.

If you have a box of stuff that hasn't been opened in years
- and you didn't need or miss anything in it -
what would make you want to keep it now?
Could you pass it on without opening it?

*Hoarding is lack of trust and fear
that there won't be enough.*

What are you hoarding?
Clothes? Money? Food?

Every morning when you wake up, say to yourself:
"Today, I have enough."

Trust that all of your needs will be met.

It is safe to let go because things don't prosper you;
Spirit prospers you.

When you look back on your life,
you may not have gotten everything you wanted but
you have probably gotten everything you needed.

When it comes to change, there is no magic bullet.
There are times when you will have to grieve the loss of
what the object represented in order to let it go.
Other times you will have to say good-bye
to the person you were and the life that you had.

Facing reality
We outgrow things;
our tastes, circumstances and lifestyles change.

Perhaps your arthritic hands will no longer allow you to knit,

or you physically can't play your favorite sport anymore,

or you've lost interest in a once cherished collection,

or your lifestyle doesn't support keeping a boat,

or you no longer attend events that require formal wear,

or you have downsized and don't have room
for your grandmother's antique bed.

Keep in mind that every time you give
yourself permission to let go,
you are making s p a c e for something new,
better or different to come into your life.

Any addiction is a sign of spiritual hunger.

Shopping addiction

You will never be able to control
the effects of seductive advertising.

The only thing you can control is you.

When you buy something that you don't need
- even if it costs you one dollar -
you have paid a much greater price.
Not only have you wasted your money
and given yourself yet another thing to take care of
(dusting, storing, fixing, etc.),
but you will have created the nuisance of either
having to return it or find another home for it.

It's interesting that we look for strength in the very substances that weaken us.

When shopping is a slippery slope:

You have packages that have never been opened.

You have things with their tags still on.

Your closets are bulging with things that you don't wear.

You shop for things that you don't need
out of boredom and frustration.

You sneak shopping bags into the house
and then hide them.

As an excuse to shop, you buy things for other people
who don't need or want more stuff.

Before consuming anything, stop and ask yourself,
"Do I really need it today?
Will it add value to my life today?
Is it going to align with what I want today?"

Just buying two things every week that you don't need will, in one year, fill your home with over one hundred items that you aren't using.

**It's probably not "things" that you want
but how it makes you feel to shop for them.**

You are your clutter, so perhaps it's time to look
at what is missing inside of your life. . .
. . . because the void you are trying to fill with things
is temporary and will never satisfy
your deep inner longing for peace.

From now on, practice conscious spending;
consider investing in things that love you back,
i.e., support your health, enrich your life
and bring timeless pleasure.

If you are renting storage s p a c e because
your home is filled to capacity, then aren't you also
contributing to our forests and fields being cleared
to erect unsightly, pre-engineered steel buildings?

*One of the most effective antidotes
to fear is a few deep breaths.*

What are you afraid of?

Is it that you might need it someday?

Fear of making a mistake?

Fear of losing control?

Yes, you might need it someday. Yes, you might make a mistake.
Yes, you might lose control. . .

. . . AND every "yes, I might. . ." is saying no
to what you want in your life.

Are you keeping something because you need it
or because you are afraid to let it go?

The past is history.
Tomorrow is a mystery.
Today is the way.

Formula for decluttering a closet
(or anything else for that matter)

1. Take everything out so you can not only see what you have but how much you have.

2. Make any repairs, paint and/or clean.

3. Sort everything into three piles:
Give away or sell
Throw away or recycle
Keep or maybe*

Now, return everything you want to keep, stand back and notice how you feel.

*Allow yourself a "maybe" pile when you can't make on-the-spot decisions.

A closet is a boundary;
so is a wallet, cupboard, room, countertop,
jewelry box, drawer, book shelf.
If they are crammed, crowded or overflowing,
you have too much stuff.

Ways to set boundaries

Set a timer and clear for 15 minutes
or eliminate 10 things every day
(a piece of paper counts as one thing).

Determine how many sweaters, plastic containers, books, etc.
you will keep and give away the rest.

Keep the best two or three
representative photographs of an event or collection.

Refrain from allowing other people to use your house
as a storage s p a c e.

Set limits on your kids' artwork, etc.
At the end of the school, have them pick their favorite
three or four pieces and let go of the rest.
This also teaches them how to set boundaries.

Limit purchases that you don't plan to use immediately.

Say no to anything that complicates your life.

*Things need to earn a right to take up
s p a c e in your home, not the other way around.*

Criteria for keeping things

Develop a criteria for keeping something.

Does it have to be. . .

beautiful
useful
wanted
loved
sentimental

? ? ?

*Spending "good" money on something
isn't a valid reason for keeping it.
While buying it may have seemed like a good idea at the time,
it isn't completing its mission of service if you aren't using or
enjoying it. The money you spent is long gone,
so cut your losses and let it go.
Pay it forward to someone who couldn't otherwise afford it.*

*Just because something was handed down
or given to you doesn't mean you have to
like it, want it or keep it.*

Other people's stuff

Their memories are not necessarily your memories.

Their taste is not your taste.

Their stuff is not your responsibility.

From now on, don't take anything from anyone
(including, and especially, your parents and relatives
because it's nearly impossible to let it go)
unless it adds value to your life.
If you do, not only is it taking up s p a c e in your home,
but now you're stuck with
the emotional, mental and physical burden
of having to part with it.

*Attraction is more effective
than promotion.*

The law of attraction

If you are living with someone who has too much stuff
- and won't part with anything -
let him or her know how their behavior is affecting you.
Share what you want and that it is important to you.
Let them know how they can support you.

Say everything you need to say
and then let it go. . .

. . . go about cleaning up your side of the street
and see what happens.

*It's not about the stuff
but our attachment to it.*

"Guilt-less" ways to pass things on

Gift a basket that you no longer want
with a nice loaf of bread
or, as a housewarming present,
recycle a vase and fill it with fresh flowers.

Throw a re-purpose party and invite
everyone you know to come and take what they want.

When possible, gift things to family members.

*If you have something that you don't like, want or need
but can't give it away, do you think the person who gave it to you
would rather you keep it hidden in storage
or exchanged for something
that would bring more pleasure into your life?
What would you want if the wheels were turned?*

*Creativity is anything that offers
a solution to the problem.*

Tangible ways
to keep a memory alive

Make a throw pillow out of your mother's wedding dress.

Take a digital photograph of your objects
to keep in a scrapbook.

Make a quilt or walling hanging from fabric squares of your
favorite things, i.e., tee shirts, a piece of your childhood blanket,
your great aunt's needlework, your father's military uniform.
Decorate with pins, photographs, metals and ribbons.
Add pictures which can be scanned and printed on fabric.

Keep one cup and saucer from your grandmother's
china collection and give away the rest.

Create a bookshelf shrine with your favorite momentos
of a person, place or event.
Take photographs of the remaining related objects
before letting them go
(the pictures can be part of the shrine).

Memories live in the heart.
Therefore, it's not possible to erase the memory of the person
when you give something away that belonged to them.

Order breeds habit.

Paper management

You will go **F.A.R.** if you remember
this acronym for handling paper...
it only goes in one of three places:

File
Action folder
Recycle

Keep an ACTION folder of "to do" things,
i.e., pay a bill, make a call,
verify a receipt for a bank statement, etc.

Once the action step has been completed, that piece of paper
either goes in a FILE or RECYCLED for the trash.

*Will your world really come crashing down
if you toss out a bank receipt,
photograph, coupon or magazine?*

Change begins at the end
of your comfort zone.

While you're clearing

Refrain from buying anything other than
necessities and consumables - food, gas and medicine.

Don't take anyone else's stuff.

Avoid watching home shopping networks
or opening catalogs that offer things you would never
knew existed unless you saw them.

Ask for gifts that can be used or consumed in one sitting such as
movie tickets, restaurant voucher, certificate for a massage.

Nothing has value if it keeps you stuck,
so keep moving through your fear, through your resistance,
through the discomfort - even when it feels like you are eliminating
options and cutting off pieces of your history -
until you can finally bless, surrender and release it. . .

. . . and then, watch a new door open.

It takes the same amount of energy
to focus on the problem as it does the solution.
Which will you choose?

Ways we slow down the process

FEAR
In order to release your fear, keep the energy moving by
identifying it, owning it, sharing it with someone, feeling it.

Solution
Ask yourself,
"What is the worst that will happen
if I give this object away?"

LACKING FOCUS
Immobilization sets in when
we see everything that has to be accomplished.

Solution
Develop "tunnel" vision by doing
one thing at a time.

CONTROL
Trying to micromanage the fate of every object
that you are giving away.

Solution
Donate your stuff to one place and trust that each thing
will find its way to the perfect person.

If you don't ask for help,
you are robbing others of giving to you.

Getting support

Partner with a friend who has a similar goal
and/or elicit help from a family member.

Hire someone who specializes in organizing.

Join a support group.

Clutter can be so overwhelming
that sometimes we can't manage it by ourselves.
While seeking support can tap into feelings of embarrassment,
not wanting to impose on others or our need to look perfect,
being humble could be the breakthrough
that you are looking for.

Motivation follows every action step.

Motivation

Anticipate bumps along the way.

Go public with your project as
other people can reinforce your behavior.

Remember the deeper meaning
for why you are doing what you are doing.

*Although the sacrifices are challenging,
they will be worth their weight in gold
when you have what you want.*

*The quality of your life depends
on the choices you make.*

Maintaining order

To create balance when buying things,
adopt the one in/one out guideline.

Instead of mindlessly shuffling papers
and other stuff from place to place or room to room,
remember the acronym for **O.H.I.O.**
- **O**nly **H**andle **I**t **O**nce -
i.e., put the object in its proper place.

Post these four simple rules where you
and your family will see them everyday:

If you take it out, put it back.
If you open it, close it.
If you throw it down, pick it up.
If you take it off, hang it up.

*Out of sight, out of mind. . .
out of control.*

Staying rid of clutter

Handle the mail when it comes in.

Become a conscious consumer.

Ask for consumable gifts.

Every time the seasons change,
go through your house and purge anything
that you no longer like, want, need or use.

*Celebrate the day when you decide to let go
and refrain from adding on.*

It's not just the sight of our stuff,
but the getting
and keeping
and maintaining
and fixing
and storing
and untangling
and tracking
that weighs us down energetically.

How to keep things looking lighter

Keep all surfaces 50% clear.

Thin out bookshelves and closets.

Hide unsightly trash cans under sinks.

Instead of piles, store things in attractive baskets.

Get things up off of the floor.

Too much clutter and you don't see anything, so think about creating more "white" s p a c e.
For example, less is more when it comes to wall art and miscellaneous stuff on your refrigerator door.

Do you own your stuff
or does your stuff own you?

The five givens of life at home

The more you have,
the more you have to take care of.

Everything gets dirty.

Mail arrives; trash accumulates and paper piles up.

It takes effort to live clutter-free.

More stuff comes in than goes out.

Everything we do in life
is a confluence of loss and gain.

Someday is not a day of the week.

Last thoughts

Whatever the object, chances are
you won't need it,
you won't fall in love with it,
you won't miss it
and you won't regret giving it away.

When it comes to changing your life for the better,
if not now, when?

It's not easy to live with only what you love, want and need;
if it were, everyone would be doing it.

How can you make peace with who you are
if you aren't content with what you have?

When it comes to making peace
with your stuff, sometimes
there's nothing left to do but let go.

About the author

Kater Leatherman's relationship with stuff changed in 1974
when she left a life of excess to live off the land in Colorado.
The experience of living polar opposite lifestyles motivated her
to explore the balance between the two.
She began to clean up her diet,
purge internal clutter and live with less stuff.

Kater's journey took her through many years of letting go
and, ultimately, personal freedom.

Today, she is a professional organizer and homestager,
leads declutter support groups,
teaches yoga and writes a monthly column
for *The Annapolis Capital*.
Her first book, *The Liberated Baby Boomer:*
Making S P A C E for Life, was published in 2008.